EDUCATION LIBRARY SERVICE

Tel: 01606 275801

KT-405-338

Robots
in Space

Steve Parker

CHESHIRE
LIBRARIES

21 MAR 2011

RL

FRANKLIN WATTS
LONDON • SYDNEY

An Appleseed Editions book

First published in 2010 by Franklin Watts
338 Euston Road, London NW1 3BH

Franklin Watts Australia
Hachette Children's Books
Level 17/207 Kent St, Sydney, NSW 2000

© 2010 Appleseed Editions

Created by Appleseed Editions Ltd,
Well House, Friars Hill, Guestling,
East Sussex TN35 4ET

Designed by Guy Callaby
Edited by Mary-Jane Wilkins
Picture research by Su Alexander

All rights reserved. No part of this publication
may be reproduced, stored in a retrieval
system or transmitted in any form or by any
means, electronic, mechanical, photocopying,
recording or otherwise, without prior
permission of the publisher.

ISBN 978 1 4451 0037 1

Dewey Classification 629.4'7

A CIP catalogue for this book is
available from the British Library.

Picture acknowledgements
title page ESA; contents ESA/D.Ducross; page 4 NASA-MSFC;
5 RIA Novosti/Alamy; 6 NASA-AMES; 7l NASA-Ames Research
Center/Eric James, r NASA-HQ-GRIN; 8 NASA/JPL-Caltech/
University of Arizona/Science Photo Library; 9t Detlev Van
Ravenswaay/Science Photo Library, b NASA/Science Photo
Library; 10 ESA, Image by C. Carreau; 11 NASA-JPL; 12t Peter
Arnold, Inc/Alamy, b NASA/JPL; 13 Warren Kovach/Alamy;
14l RIA Novosti/Alamy, r NASA courtesy Northrop Grumman;
15 NASA; 16 ESA; 17 NASA-KSC; 18 NASA-MSFC; 19t RIA
Novosti/Alamy, b NASA-HQ-GRIN; 20 ESA/D.Ducross;
21t Chris Butler/Science Photo Library, b NASA-JPL; 22t JAXA,
b Johns Hopkins University Applied Physics Laboratory/
Science Photo Library; 23 Detlev Van Ravenswaay/Science
Photo Library; 24 ESA-NASA; 25t ESA/D.Ducross, b NASA;
26 NASA-JPL; 27 JHUAPL/SWRI/NASA/Science Photo Library;
28 William K. Hartmann,UCLA/NASA/Science Photo Library;
29t NASA-KSC, b NASA/Science Photo Library
Front cover NASA/Science Photo Library

Printed in China

Franklin Watts is a division of Hachette
Children's Books,
an Hachette UK company.
www.hachette.co.uk

Contents

Robots blast off!

Very few people go into space. To become an astronaut you have to train for years. It must be amazing to look down on planet Earth spinning slowly below, and to look up at distant planets, moons and stars. But robots do this every day!

A space shuttle launch is exciting for people on board, but just another day for the robots.

ROBOT OR NOT?

Rocket-bot?

*Is a space rocket a robot? Not really. It can travel about, has moving parts and controls itself to some extent. But we call rockets launch vehicles rather than true robots. We use the name robot to describe some of the machines that rockets carry, such as wheeled **rovers** or remote-control **landers** that touch down on a planet.*

Danger, danger!

Space is a dangerous place. There's no air to breathe, no food or drink – in fact, nothing at all. Travelling somewhere interesting such as a planet takes months or even years. When you get there, it might be too cold or hot to survive. If your spacecraft breaks down, help is a long way away.

Equipped to cope

None of this worries a robot. Most robots are machines made of metals, plastics and similar materials. They don't need air, water or food, although they do need energy to keep them going – usually electricity. They have no feelings, so they don't feel lonely or frightened.

Small and simple

A spacecraft carrying people needs food, drinks and other supplies. It must have safety equipment and back-up systems. The craft has to be able to withstand enormous heat as it re-enters the **atmosphere** (the thick layer of air around the Earth) to bring the astronauts home. A spacecraft carrying a robot needs no supplies. It can be smaller and lighter, so it needs a smaller rocket for lift-off, and it costs less too.

ROBOT SUPERSTAR

Lunokhod 1
The first robot to land on another world was Lunokhod 1 from Russia. It was carried by the spacecraft Luna 17 and touched down on the Moon in 1970. It was 2.3 metres long and had eight wheels and two television camera eyes. Guided from Earth by remote control Lunokhod was a great success. In 11 months it travelled more than ten km and took 20,000 close-up pictures.

On Earth and in space

Are space robots the same as robots on Earth? In many ways, yes. Most robots are partly automatic. They can make simple decisions and work on their own for a time. Most robots have parts that move, such as levers and motors. Some can travel about on wheels or bendy legs. All these features make them ideal for work in space.

Robots need people

Robots carry out tasks for us. They may be very clever, especially the latest types with computer brains. But they cannot work on their own all the time. They need instructions or programs from us, otherwise they do not know what to do. Also something might happen that a robot is not programmed to deal with. Then a person has to take control of the robot and decide what to do.

▼ *Robots designed to drill into the Moon or Mars are tested in the bone-chilling cold of the Arctic region.*

Robo-blog■

BRRRRRR!

'I'm being tested near the North Pole and today was the coldest I've ever been. It's minus 30 degrees here and my wheels nearly froze. The wind almost blew me over. My batteries are weak and my headlights are dim. Luckily my human masters can fix it all. If happened when I got to the Moon, I'd be a dead-bot!'■

The K10 Mars rover can 'see' into the ground with its very powerful radar that uses strong radio waves.

Emergency repairs

When a robot breaks down on Earth, someone can usually mend it, but if a robot breaks down in deep space, there will be no one around to fix it. So space-bots must be designed very carefully. They need lots of back-up equipment and reserve systems to make sure that if one part fails, another can take over. They have to be tested in the most extreme conditions they might encounter.

DO YOU KNOW?

(ROBOTS DO)

How much am I?

How much do space robots cost? It's difficult to say. There's the cost of the robot itself, its design and development and testing. There's also the cost of the rocket which launches it, and the control and communications centre here on Earth. For the two Mars rovers Spirit and Opportunity (see page 17) the total cost was $410 million (about £285 million) each. That's cheap compared with sending people into space, which would cost hundreds of times more!

A space-bot on Mercury, the closest planet to the Sun, would endure temperatures of more than 400°C – much hotter than an oven (see page 19).

Electro-bots

Most robots are powered by electricity. But far away in space there are no mains sockets where we can plug in a robot to recharge its batteries. So how do space robots keep going?

Using electricity

Electricity is the most convenient way to power a robot. Most robots store instructions and information in microchips and memory discs powered by electricity. Electricity also drives the motors that move the robot's parts. But space travel can last for months or even years and the most powerful batteries would run down. So space robots must be able to recharge their batteries.

Sun power

Robots that are not too far from the Sun can use its light to make electricity. They have **solar panels** very similar to the panels we use on Earth, which capture the energy in sunlight and turn it into electricity. These panels are big, to catch enough light. They are usually folded up while the robot is launched into space. Once it is in space the solar panels open out (or are deployed).

Help for Earth

*Every year scientists make solar panels that are better, or more efficient, at turning sunlight into electricity. This research helps space robots – and also improves the way we use solar power here on Earth. If we make electricity using solar power, we need to make less electricity by burning **fossil fuels** in power stations. So using solar power helps to combat **global warming**.*

After the Phoenix lander touched down on Mars in May 2008 it opened its solar panels, which are about the same size as a double bed.

Mars is further from the Sun than we are, so the Sun looks smaller and dimmer from there. Scientists need to allow for this when they design solar panels for Martian space-bots.

Deep space darkness

Away from the Sun, beyond the planet Mars, the sunlight is too weak to charge solar panels. So deep-space robots have a device called an **RTG**. The initials stand for radio-isotope thermoelectric generator. This machine uses a specially-made lump of a radioactive substance for fuel, such as **plutonium**. It gives off rays and radiation that warm sets of wires made of different metals, called **thermocouples**. The heat makes electricity flow through the wires to charge the batteries. RTGs can produce (or generate) electricity for years at a time.

ROBOT SUPERSTAR

Pioneer 11

Robot probe
Pioneer 11 was launched in 1973 on an immensely long journey past the giant planets Jupiter and Saturn, and on into deepest space. Its radio signals continued for more than 22 years until its four shoebox-sized SNAP-19 RTGs finally became too weak to make enough electricity.

Senses in space

We send space robots on great journeys for many reasons. We want to discover what other worlds are like, such as distant planets or moons. Is the surface covered with diamonds? Are there aliens? Could people survive there? To send us the information we want, space robots need **sensors** – cameras to see, microphones to hear, 'hands' to touch and feel, and many other sensing devices.

Space science

Space robots don't go on trips just to satisfy our curiosity. Scientists want specific information about other worlds, such as the temperature there, what the surface rocks and dust are like, and whether there is any air. This information helps them to understand how planets, stars and other objects formed long ago, and how they might end in the distant future.

In 2008 deep-space traveller Rosetta passed near to the asteroid Steins and took pictures with its telescopic and wide-angle cameras (see page 23).

What do robots see?

Nearly all space robots have a camera. In fact, most have more than one. Many of these cameras take still pictures. Others record videos or movies. The digital cameras change the patterns of light rays into electronic digital codes and send these to Earth by radio waves. Some cameras look through telescopes to get close-up views. Others have wide-angle lenses to show the bigger picture.

▶▶ *Outermost planet Neptune has been visited only once, by Voyager 2 in 1989. It sent back wonderful colour pictures of this mysterious deep-blue world.*

What they measure

Space robots have many other sensors apart from cameras. Thermometers check the temperature, **gravity** detectors measure the force (or pull) of gravity, radio receivers record natural radio waves sent out by stars, and **magnetometers** measure the magnetic forces around a planet or moon. All this scientific information helps us to understand more about space and about our own planet Earth.

▼ *In 1995 the Galileo robo-craft mapped the giant planet Jupiter, taking pictures with infrared light that our own eyes cannot see.*

DO YOU KNOW?

(ROBOTS DO)

I can see you!

*Human eyes can't see the types of light called **ultraviolet** or **infrared**. But many space robots can. They have special cameras that take pictures using these types of light rays. Computers can then turn the information into pictures human eyes can see.*

Talking to space-bots

The fastest speed in the universe is the **speed of light**, which is 300,000 kilometres per second. The radio signals we send and receive from space robots are similar to light rays, and they travel at the same speed. But space is so vast, even that's not fast enough.

Robo-comms

We use radio communications to talk and listen to space robots. Scientists send them instructions as radio signals telling them what to switch on and turn off, where to point their cameras, and where to go. The robots send information back to Earth about what their cameras see and all the things they measure.

As space robots journey to the edge of our solar system, radio signals take several hours to travel to and from Earth. This is called communication lag.

Be careful

For some space robots, this time delay causes problems. It's not possible for someone on Earth to drive a robot rover on Mars by remote control. If the person sees through the camera that the rover is heading for a rock, and steers away, the signals could take almost an hour to reach the rover. So robot rovers explore very slowly. Some have touch sensors to feel objects, and a computer that recognizes anything which might be in the way.

▶▶ *The Sojourner rover on Mars used laser beams to detect things in the way (see page 17).*

A long delay

Here on Earth, distances are so small that radio signals bring television programmes to your aerial or dish in fractions of a second. Signals take just over a second to travel to the Moon. Mars is a lot further away. Even when it is nearest to Earth in its **orbit** (journey around the Sun), radio signals take more than five minutes to travel there. When Mars is on the other side of the Sun from us, signals take more than 20 minutes. Signals to and from the *Cassini* robot probe, which is going around the distant planet Saturn, take more than an hour to arrive.

ROBO-FUTURE

Sub-space messages

Scientists have many ideas about whether some kinds of rays or waves could travel faster than light. If so, they would make 'sub-space' communications possible, so that radio signals travelled along them in just seconds rather than hours.

Giant radio dishes receive the amazingly weak signals from space robots and radio back instructions to them.

Robo-blog■

VERY LONELY

'I haven't talked to my friends on Earth for two weeks. The planet I've landed on spins very slowly, and at the moment, the place I am in faces away from Earth. So I can't send or receive any radio signals. Never mind. I've got plenty of pictures to take and things to measure. That will have to do for now I suppose ...'■

Off to the Moon

Some people love the idea of visiting another world, such as the Moon or Mars, to live there for a time. Before humans could build a living base there, we would have to send robots to find a good site and check for problems.

DO YOU KNOW?

(ROBOTS DO)

Wrong place!
Even touching down on another world is very dangerous. You might land on a steep cliff, a big boulder or in a pile of deep dust. It's best to send a robot scout to find the safest landing area before people travel there.

Looking up close
The LRO, or Lunar Reconnaissance Orbiter, is a robot **satellite** which goes around the Moon studying its surface. Its powerful telescope cameras see mountains and valleys, cliffs, boulders, and flat dusty plains in great detail. LRO can look into craters to detect any signs of frozen water, which would be very useful for people living in a Moon base.

▼ *In 1976 Lunar 24 brought samples of Moon dust and rock back to Earth, to see whether they could be any help for a Moon base.*

I saw the bang
LCROSS is a special robot that watched a space rocket plunge to its death! It was launched by the same rocket as LRO and its cameras saw the rocket smash into the Moon at more than 9000 kilometres per hour. Scientists can study pictures of the explosion, the hole or crater it made, and the dust it threw up, to learn more about the Moon's surface.

This version of Scarab is a prototype or trial model. It's for testing on Earth in Moon-like places such as soft sand, steep hills and boulder-covered plains.

Scouting about

Another Moon robot is Scarab, a four-wheeled rover the size of a sports car. There is plenty of sunshine on the Moon, but Scarab is designed to explore deep, dark craters, so it has an RTG for electricity (see page 9). It can find its own way using laser beams and an on-board computer – and it can drill! It can lower itself down on to its underside and send a drill one metre down into the rocks, to look for ice, water, minerals and any other useful substances.

ROBOT OR NOT?

Sat-bot?

Is a satellite in space a robot? In most cases, not really. It does a simple job for us, such as beaming down TV programmes or taking photographs. But a satellite does not usually have moving parts, and it cannot make decisions for itself, whereas many space robots can.

Let's go to Mars!

Mars is the most visited place in space after our Moon. More than 40 robot craft have passed nearby, gone into orbit or landed on the surface. But Mars is also a risky place to visit. More than half of all Mars missions have run into trouble or failed completely. Some people say that's because of **sabotage** by **Martians**!

The ExoMars rover plans to land on the Red Planet sometime after 2013. It will search for water, signs of life and useful minerals and substances (see page 29).

DO YOU KNOW?

(ROBOTS DO)

Lost forever?

*Late in 2003 the Mars lander Beagle 2 left its orbiting **mothercraft**, Mars Express, and headed down to the surface, then all radio contact was lost. No one knows whether it landed or not, or if it was destroyed. But maybe a robot somewhere knows?*

Nine-year-old Sofi Collis won a competition to name the two Mars rovers, with her suggestions of Spirit and Opportunity. Before that they were called MER-1 and MER-2.

Failure, success

The first space robots to land on Mars were Mars 2 and Mars 3 in 1971. But scientists on Earth lost radio contact with them as they touched down. Much more successful were the Viking 1 and Viking 2 landers in 1976. They couldn't move around, but they had cameras and other sensors, including wind and earthquake detectors. They carried out chemical tests to see if there was any life, but they found nothing.

Roving about

In 1997 *Mars Pathfinder* sent down a lander that released a skateboard-sized robot rover, Sojourner. It spent three months driving about, photographing the rocks and scenery, and analysing the soil (see photo on page 12). Once again, it found no Martian life. Like many other robot space rovers, Sojourner finally lost all electrical power. It's still there on Mars, silent and still and 'asleep'.

Still nothing

The Phoenix lander arrived on Mars in May 2008. It was the size of a small truck, with big solar panels, springy legs and equipment to measure the weather, soil and rocks. As the Martian winter came there was no longer enough sunlight for its solar panels, and its mission finished in November. Again it found no signs of life.

ROBOT SUPERSTAR

Spirit and Opportunity

In 2004 two rovers began to explore different areas of Mars. Spirit and Opportunity have been a huge success, lasting 20 times longer than planned, covering dozens of kilometres and sending back thousands of pictures. They have even ground up rocks to study.

Red hot planets

The closest planet to Earth is Venus. It's a mysterious world, covered in thick clouds of poison gases and acid drops. Humans could never survive there and even space robots have problems.

Hotter than two ovens

The temperature on Venus is 460° Celsius – more than twice as hot as an oven. The thick gases of the atmosphere on Venus have a pressure almost 100 times the **air pressure** here on Earth. So this planet has presented a huge challenge to space robot designers.

▼ *Through a telescope, the planet Venus looks like a giant swirling blob. Space robots have travelled down to see its rocky, mountainous surface.*

DO YOU KNOW?

(ROBOTS DO)

Mystery loss

The first robot spacecraft to reach the surface of another planet was Venera 3 *in 1966. At least, that's what scientists think. Radio contact was lost as it arrived. So it was probably damaged by a crash-landing. But who knows what really happened?*

Many visitors

From the 1960s to the 1980s a long series of *Venera* robot probes touched down on Venus and sent back pictures and other information. In 1978 the *Pioneer Venus Multiprobe* included five mini-robots. The *Magellan* space-bot orbited Venus from 1989 to 1994 and *Venus Express* arrived in 2006. Both of these have **radar** equipment that can see through the thick clouds to map the surface.

Almost on fire

Mercury is the closest planet to the Sun, and its surface temperature reaches 430° Celsius. It has only been visited once by a robot space mission, *Mariner 10*, in 1975. A second robot visit is planned by *Messenger*, which was launched in 2004 and should arrive in 2011. That's a very long time to travel to a relatively close planet. This is because Mercury is so near the Sun that the Sun's huge gravity tries to pull a space robot into its fiery surface. So *Messenger* has to approach very carefully and use its **thrusters** to brake hard and slow down.

▼ *SOHO, the Solar and Heliospheric Observatory, has 12 measuring instruments that study the hottest object around – the Sun, whose surface is 6000° Celsius.*

ROBOT OR NOT?

Floating robots

In 1985 the Vega *Mission sent two landers to Venus, and also two balloons! Each balloon was about 3.4 metres across and floated for more than 40 hours through the thick **acid clouds**. Their packs of science equipment took measurements such as temperature, wind speed and pressure. Are such balloons true robots? Their official name is autonomous flying robots or aerobots.*

Exploring together

Many space missions involve not just one robot, but two or more working as a team. A common combination is an orbiter and a lander. The orbiter goes round and round the planet or moon, and releases the lander to touch down on the surface.

Seven-year trip

The greatest robot team so far to explore space is *Cassini* and Huygens. They set off together in 1997 to the giant planet Saturn with its beautiful rings. They took almost seven years to reach Saturn's orbit. In early 2005 the lander Huygens left the **orbiter** *Cassini* and plunged towards the surface – but not Saturn's surface. Its target was Saturn's massive moon Titan.

Robo-blog■

THE COLDEST PLACE

'It's so c-c-c-old. I hope they remember me back home on Earth. I almost cried when I left my best friend Cassini to come down here on to freezing, super-windy Titan. My thermometer says its minus 180°! Still, I've done my best. I hope the robots of the future will be inspired by my efforts. G-g-g-g-goodbye...'■

▼ *Huygens' heat shield glowed as it hurtled down into Titan's atmosphere, then fell away. Two parachutes, one after the other, slowed it down further. Huygens landed at a speed of five metres per second – as fast as a human runs.*

ROBO-FUTURE

Massive moons

Space scientists are always planning the next mission for their robots. The Europa Jupiter System Mission aims to blast off in 2020 to the biggest planet, Jupiter, to explore its four massive moons Io, Europa, Ganymede and Callisto.

Careful timing

Like *Cassini*, Titan orbits around Saturn. Space scientists had to make sure that *Cassini*, Titan and Huygens all moved into the best positions for the landing. There was only a short time period during which this could happen, as with many space missions. A mistake would have spelled disaster for the robot team.

Hurtling Huygens

For two and a half hours Huygens plunged through the atmosphere of Titan, protected by a heat shield and slowed by two parachutes. During the descent and for 90 minutes afterwards, it sent back more than 350 pictures by radio, as well as information about Titan's winds, weather and icy surface. Small Huygens sent radio signals to bigger *Cassini*, then *Cassini*'s more powerful radio equipment sent them on, or relayed them, all the way back to Earth.

▲ *Huygens' target was Titan, here on the right, with ringed Saturn in the background. Titan is so huge it has its own atmosphere. Parachutes only work if there is an atmosphere.*

▼ *The orbiter* Cassini *has taken thousands of pictures of Saturn and its moons Titan (three views are shown here), Rhea, Iapetus and others. Its mission will last at least 14 years.*

Small strange worlds

Apart from planets and moons, there are other objects for space robots to visit. They include asteroids and **comets**. These have their own special hazards. Asteroids tumble and turn as they zoom through space, so it's difficult to land on them. Comets grow very hot when they're near the Sun and squirt out powerful, volcano-like blasts of gases.

Soft landing

Asteroids are chunks of rock travelling around the Sun, which are too small to be planets. Various robot craft, such as *Mariner 9*, *Galileo* and *Deep Space 1*, have flown near asteroids and photographed them. The first to go very near an asteroid was *Near Earth Asteroid Rendezvous – Shoemaker*, usually called *NEAR-Shoemaker*. It was launched in 1996, flew close to asteroid Mathilde in 1997, then orbited and finally soft-landed on asteroid Eros in 2001. It took pictures and made measurements for about two weeks before it went to 'sleep'.

DO YOU KNOW?

(ROBOTS DO)

Trouble in space

A deep space robot called Hayabusa has had troubles on its travels. It set off in 2003 to land on the asteroid Itokawa and gather samples of rock and dust to bring back to Earth. But its football-sized mini-lander drifted away, its balancing equipment broke, its thrusters jammed and its landing went wrong. Scientists hope it may still come back to Earth, but no one yet knows whether it has any samples.

▼ *Robot craft NEAR-Shoemaker **approaches asteroid Eros, preparing to touch down. Finding Eros in the vast depths of space was an amazing feat – it is just 30 kilometres long.***

Not so soft

A space robot made a far harder landing on a comet five years later. Comets are balls of ice and dust that come from far outside the planets, loop around the Sun and head away again, glowing as they pass. In 2005 Comet Tempel 1 came quite close to Earth, so space robot *Deep Impact* went to meet it. After studying and photographing it, *Deep Impact* released a section called an impactor that slammed into Tempel 1, causing an explosion equal to one made by igniting five tonnes of dynamite. *Deep Impact* and telescopes here on Earth recorded the collision to find out what comets are made of.

The fridge-sized impactor from Deep Impact made a crater 100 metres wide in Comet Tempel 1. The comet flashed briefly, shining six times more brightly than usual.

ROBO-FUTURE

Far into the future

In 2004 the mothercraft Rosetta (see photo page 10) and its robot lander Philae took off for Comet Churyumov-Gerasimenko. It's a long trip, and they should arrive in 2014. On the way they are flying past asteroids Steins (visited in 2008) and Lutetia (2010).

23

International Space Station

Not all space robots go on long journeys among the planets. Some stay quite close to Earth and do regular jobs, such as taking supplies to the the International Space Station.

Space ferries

The International Space Station – or ISS – orbits about 350 kilometres above Earth's surface, going once around the planet every 91 minutes. Spacecraft such as *Soyuz* and space shuttles carry people to and from it. There are also ISS robo-ferries or space trucks. These are robotic craft that work on their own, with no crew. They are launched by rockets and fly to the ISS with food, water, fuel, tools and scientific equipment. These robots also take new parts so that astronauts can continue building the ISS, which will not be finished for several years.

Building work on the ISS, codenamed Alpha, began in 1998. Dozens of robot craft have carried up new parts to fix on to it.

Only used once

The most regular robot ferries are Progress freighters. They are similar to the *Soyuz* craft which has carried crew members up into space and back for many years. About four Progress craft go to the ISS every year. They are always new, because they are destroyed once they have completed their tasks. Each craft travels to the ISS with more than two tonnes of supplies and automatically attaches itself or docks to the ISS. It is unloaded and then filled with waste. Then it leaves the space station, heads back to Earth – and burns up on re-entry into the atmosphere.

Auto space truck

In 2008 another automatic space truck joined the ISS team. This is the **ATV**, Automated Transfer Vehicle. It is bigger than a Progress freighter and has up to ten tonnes of supplies and a complicated computer that controls its approach and docking with the ISS. Like Progress, every ATV self-destructs – it burns up on its way back to Earth.

▶▶ *The Ariane 5 rocket's nose opens to release the ATV robot ferry on its way to the ISS. Its cargo includes food, water, oxygen, thruster fuel, clothes and science experiments.*

ROBOT SUPERSTAR

Dextre

In 2008 a two-armed robot called Dextre was sent to the ISS. Its full name is the Special Purpose Dexterous Manipulator (SPDM). It has two movable arms, each more than three metres long, and a three-metre-long body. The arms have hand-like grabs that bend and twist. Dextre stays outside the ISS and carries out tasks such as fixing on new pieces brought by Progress and ATV. This means human crew members do not have to take a spacewalk outside.

The longest journey

Pluto is a long, long way away from Earth. This **dwarf planet** is at the edge of the solar system and has not been visited by any space robots – yet. The greatest robo-traveller of our time, *New Horizons*, is on its way there.

▼ *Even seen through a very powerful telescope, Pluto looks tiny from Earth. It is just one object in the vast jumble of stars and planets.*

DO YOU KNOW?

(ROBOTS DO)

Fastest ever

New Horizons zoomed away from Earth at more than 58,000 kilometres per hour – the fastest object ever to leave our planet. Maybe robots compare their speeds to see who is quickest, slowest, heaviest, or most tired...

Endless mission

New Horizons left Earth in January 2006. Just over a year later it passed Jupiter, then in 2008 it whizzed past Saturn's orbit. But Pluto is so far away that it won't arrive there until 2015. After studying the dwarf planet and its big moon Charon, *New Horizons* will go on, and on, as long as scientists on Earth can track it and stay in contact.

Waiting and waiting...

New Horizons is almost the size of a car and has a very big radio dish. Eventually it will be so far from Earth that its radio signals become very weak, and they will take four hours to arrive here. Its five packs of science equipment include a powerful telescope camera, a close-up camera and a dust collector. Like all deep-space robots, *New Horizons* has an RTG to make its electricity (see page 9).

New grows old

New Horizons is on such a long journey that by the time it reaches to Pluto in 2015 it will seem old and out of date. Scientists started building it in 1998 and spent years designing and testing it. In the meantime, technology on Earth advances almost every week, as computers grow faster and more powerful. Space scientists need to make sure that the latest equipment here can still receive signals from space robots that were built ten or even 20 years ago.

▲ *As* New Horizons *flew past Jupiter it took close-up pictures of the planet and many of its moons, including hundreds of active volcanoes on the moon Io.*

Robo-blog■

TIME FOR A NAP

'That's the Jupiter flypast done. I saw some spectacular views of the giant planet and its moons. Now it's time for a nap. As I hop between the planets, I close down many of my circuits and systems to save power. I send back the occasional signal to Earth to let them know all is well. After that, it's robo-snoring time. Zzzzz.'■

Infinity and beyond

Space scientists are never short of ideas for new robots and other craft that will go faster, travel further, take more pictures and gather more information about our world and the universe.

On its way

The *Dawn* space robot is aiming for several firsts. It will be first to visit the asteroid Vesta and the dwarf planet Ceres (formerly called an asteroid) in the Asteroid Belt, between Mars and Jupiter. This is a very long way away – *Dawn* blasted off in 2007, but will not reach Vesta until 2012 and Ceres in 2015. *Dawn* has special new engines called xenon ion thrusters. Usually robotic spacecraft that visit two places simply fly past the first, without going into orbit. But *Dawn* will use its **ion engines** to power out of orbit around Vesta and head on to Ceres.

▲ *Dawn's main body or 'bus' is about the size of a small car and its radio dish is 1.5 metres across. It measures almost 20 metres in length, including its solar panels.*

Stardust

In 2006 Stardust returned to Earth's orbit after a journey of seven years and five billion kilometres. This space robot had a part which looked like a big, sticky tennis racquet that folded out as it whizzed past Comet Wild 2, to collect tiny bits of space dust from the comet. The dust samples came back to Earth's surface in a re-entry container that landed by parachute. Stardust boosted away from Earth into deep space. It showed that deep-space 'sample return' missions can be successful, and now more are planned.

◀◀ *Stardust is prepared for launch in 1999. The brown and white cake-like part on top is the return capsule that landed back on Earth.*

Robo-astronaut

Most space robots look nothing like humans because they are designed to do jobs that humans can't do. Robonaut is human-shaped, with movable arms and hands, and five fingers. It has been designed to take over tasks once carried out by astronauts in spacesuits. Each arm and hand has more than 150 sensors for touch, position and temperature, as well as force of movement and grip.

▶▶ *Robonaut is an android, which means it's a robot with a human-like shape.*

ROBO-FUTURE

The cleverest yet

Several space robots have searched for life on Mars without success. Could ExoMars find it? This robot space probe will have an orbiter, a lander and a rover similar to Spirit or Opportunity. The ExoMars rover will be the most intelligent space-bot ever, able to find its own way, steer around obstacles, and 'sniff' for signs of life. But it will not be ready for a long time – its launch is planned for after 2013.

Glossary of robo-terms

acid clouds
Clouds made of tiny floating drops of acid chemicals, which burn and eat away things they touch.

air pressure
The pressing force of the invisible floating gases in the air or atmosphere around us on Earth.

asteroid
A large lump of rock in space travelling around the Sun, which is not big enough to be a proper planet and which does not give off gases, unlike a comet.

atmosphere
The layer of gases around a large space object such as a star, planet or big moon. It usually grows thinner the higher it is above the surface.

ATV
Automatic Transfer Vehicle, a robot spacecraft that travels from Earth with no crew to join the International Space Station.

comet
A lump of mixed rock, dust and ice in space going around the Sun, which gives off gases and dust when it is warmed near the Sun.

dwarf planet
A lump of rock in space which is too small to be a proper planet but too large to be an asteroid.

fossil fuels
Substances we burn for heat, which are the preserved remains of plants and other living things from millions of years ago. The main ones are coal, oil (petroleum) and natural gas.

global warming
The gradual heating up of Earth due to increasing amounts of certain gases in its atmosphere, especially carbon dioxide, which is produced by burning fossil fuels and other fuels.

gravity
The natural pulling force that all objects have, from pieces of dust to stars, that attracts other objects. The bigger or more massive an object, the stronger its gravity.

infrared light
Light with waves slightly longer than red light waves, which our eyes cannot see, but which some cameras and other sensors can detect.

ion engine
An engine similar to a rocket engine but much weaker, which uses electrical and magnetic forces to move tiny particles called ions and cause a push or thrust.

lander
A spacecraft designed to touch down or land without damage on another world (planet, moon, asteroid or comet) and carry out measurements and experiments.

magnetometer
A device that measures the magnetic field or magnetic force around an object, from a simple fridge magnet to a whole moon, planet or star.

Martian
To do with Mars, for example, Martian rocks are those on Mars or which have come from Mars.

mothercraft
A larger spacecraft to which a smaller craft or probe is attached. It usually carries the smaller craft to a certain place and releases it for its mission.

orbit
Going round and round a larger object on a regular path or track.

orbiter
A spacecraft designed to orbit a large space object such as a planet, moon, asteroid or comet, rather than fly past it or land on it.

plutonium
A rare heavy metal substance that gives off rays and radiation including heat rays.

radar
Sending out radio signals and detecting them when they bounce back off an object, to show the size, shape and distance of the object.

radio telescope
A telescope that detects radio waves and similar invisible waves, rather than light rays.

robot probe
A robot craft without a crew that carries out a task in space.

rover
In space exploration, a vehicle or buggy that moves around under its own power, usually on wheels.

RTG
Radio-isotope thermal generator, a device that makes electricity from heat, using a substance such as plutonium for fuel.

sabotage
Doing something deliberately to cause a problem, failure or breakdown.

satellite
An object that goes around, or orbits, another one. The Moon is a natural satellite of Earth. Sometimes the word is used to mean man-made objects rather than natural ones.

sensor
A device that detects and measures something, such as a camera for light, a microphone for sound and a magnetometer for magnetic forces.

solar panels
Large flat surfaces containing many small electrical gadgets called solar cells that turn light energy into electricity.

speed of light
About 300,000 kilometres per second, the fastest speed in the universe, not only for light but for radio waves, X-rays and similar rays and waves.

thermocouples
Lengths of wires made from different metals joined together end to end. Electricity flows through the wires when they are heated.

thrusters
Small rocket-like engines that puff out spurts of gas to make a spacecraft twist around or change its position.

ultraviolet light
Light with waves slightly shorter than violet light waves, which our eyes cannot see, but which some cameras can detect.

Further reading

Robots by Clive Gifford (Carlton Books 2008)

Building Robots with LEGO Mindstorms NXT
by Mario Ferrari (Syngress 2007)

Robot by Roger Bridgman (DK Eyewitness Books 2004)

Learn About Robotics (Sci Faxes)
by De-Ann Black (Top That! 2005)

Robots and Robotics series:
How Robots Work and other titles
Tony Hyland (Macmillan Library, Nelson Thornes 2008)

Ultimate Robot by Robert Malone (Dorling Kindersley 2004)

Websites

Robot World News
This site covers the top news stories on robotics, artificial intelligence and related areas, but it also has more fun information on robots such as toys.
http://www.robotworldnews.com/robots4u.html

Robot video clips
Video clips of all kinds of robots in action.
http://www.robotclips.com/

Robot Wars
In the popular Robot Wars competitions, teams strive to improve robots of all kinds, not just for battle – see especially the SAFETY page.
http://www.ukrobotwars.com/mains.htm

Index